SOCIAL
MEDIA
SENSATIONS

Instagram

Joanne Mattern

Checkerboard Library

An Imprint of Abdo Publishing
abdopublishing.com

Printed in the United States of America, North Mankato, Minnesota
062016
092016

 THIS BOOK CONTAINS RECYCLED MATERIALS

Design: Emily Love, Mighty Media, Inc.
Production: Mighty Media, Inc.
Editor: Liz Salzmann
Cover Photos: Kelly Doudna, Shutterstock
Interior Photos: Alamy, p. 21; AP Images, pp. 5, 9, 11, 17; iStockphoto, p. 19; Kelly Doudna, pp. 14, 15; Shutterstock, pp. 7, 13, 15, 23, 25, 26, 27, 29; Wikimedia Commons, 4

Publishers Cataloging-in-Publication Data
Names: Mattern, Joanne, author.
Title: Instagram / by Joanne Mattern.
Description: Minneapolis, MN : Abdo Publishing, [2017] | Series: Social media sensations | Includes index.
Identifiers: LCCN 2016934274 | ISBN 9781680781908 (lib. bdg.) |
    ISBN 9781680775754 (ebook)
Subjects: LCSH: Online social networks--Juvenile literature. | Photography--Digital techniques--Juvenile literature. | Image processing--Digital techniques--Juvenile literature. | Internet industry--United States--Juvenile literature.
Classification: DDC 775--dc23
LC record available at /http://lccn.loc.gov/2016934274

Contents

Instagram

URL: https://instagram.com

PURPOSE: Instagram is a photo- and video-sharing website. Users can upload photos and videos and comment on them.

CURRENT CEO: Kevin Systrom

NUMBER OF USERS: More than 400 million

OCTOBER 6, 2010
Instagram is founded

APRIL 9, 2012
Facebook buys Instagram

JUNE 20, 2013
Instagram Videos are introduced

DECEMBER 12, 2013
Instagram Direct is introduced

Meet the Founders

KEVIN SYSTROM was born on December 30, 1983. He grew up in Holliston, Massachusetts. Systrom went to Stanford University in California. He worked for several Internet start-ups before founding Instagram with Mike Krieger. Systrom met Krieger at Stanford.

MIKE KRIEGER was born in Sao Paulo, Brazil, on March 4, 1986. In high school, he taught computer skills to adults after school. Later, Krieger came to the United States to study at Stanford University. Like Systrom, Krieger worked for a start-up firm before creating Instagram.

Mike Krieger

Kevin Systrom

CHAPTER 1

What Is Instagram?

You take a photo of a beautiful sunset. You use *filters* to make the photo look even more amazing. Then you post the photo on Instagram. Your followers see the photo and comment on how great it looks. Their followers can then see your photo too. Soon, it's being viewed by people around the world. This is the power of Instagram!

Instagram is a photo- and video-sharing website. Users learn more about people they follow through visual posts. Users post everything from images of important life events to funny pet photos.

Users can also comment on other's posts. This

Did You Know?

One of the most popular pictures on Instagram is of model Kendall Jenner. In the photo, she is lying on the floor with her hair arranged in heart shapes. The photo received 2.5 million likes in just five weeks.

Instagram's filters set it apart from other photo-sharing sites. Using a filter can give a photo an artistic touch.

interaction is a big part of Instagram. It has become a very popular way for people to share moments from their daily lives using photography.

CHAPTER 2

Instagram Is Born

Kevin Systrom is a cofounder of Instagram. In 2009, Systrom worked for a travel website called Nextstop. While there, he had an idea to build his own app. Systrom's app allowed people to use a mobile device's Global Positioning System (GPS) to tell others where they were. Users could also play games and share pictures on the app.

Systrom called his app Burbn. He then asked Mike Krieger to work on Burbn with him. The two had met years earlier, as classmates at Stanford University in California. Krieger agreed to help build the app.

Burbn launched in March 2010. The founders soon realized people most often used the app's photo-sharing function. So Systrom and Krieger created a new app just for sharing photos taken on mobile phones.

The new app had special tools for editing photos. It also allowed users to caption their images and comment

Systrom (left) works with engineer Shayne Sweeney (center) and Krieger (right) at Instagram's San Francisco, California, headquarters in 2011.

on others' photos. Systrom and Krieger called the app Instagram, a combination of the words *instant* and *telegram*. Instagram was launched on October 6, 2010.

CHAPTER 3

Instagram Takes Off

Upon Instagram's launch, people immediately loved it! By December 2010, Instagram had 1 million users. Systrom and Krieger could barely keep the servers running fast enough to support the app.

Instagram continued to grow quickly. The 150 millionth photo was uploaded on August 3, 2011. About one month later, Instagram reached 10 million users.

Celebrities were quick to adopt Instagram. This helped the app grow even faster. Singers, actors, and athletes saw it as a way to connect with their fans. For fans, following their favorite celebrities' photos was like having windows into their lives.

Companies saw Instagram as a way to interact with consumers. The app had a search engine so users could search for images by keywords or themes. This allowed companies to use Instagram as a database where

The 150 millionth Instagram photo was this image of people on a swing ride at a carnival.

consumers could search for items to buy. Companies also encouraged consumers to like their photos. This helped promote the companies and their products.

CHAPTER 4

Sharing and Tagging

Whether individuals or companies, all Instagram users create photo-sharing communities on the site. When a user uploads a photo, it is shared with all of his or her followers. The followers can then share the photo with their followers by liking or commenting on it. As more users interact with the photo, it is shared again and again.

Tagging is another way to share photos with others. Instagram users can tag other users in their photos. This means they include the other users' usernames in the photo captions or comments. The tagged users get notified, and their followers see the image too.

Hashtags are another kind of tag. Hashtags can be included in image captions or comments. These are keywords placed after a hash symbol (#). For example, a photo of friends at a beach may have the tags #ocean, #friendsatthebeach, and more. Once these tags are

This photo might include the hashtags #fashion and #friends. These are two of the top Instagram hashtags.

placed, users can find the images by searching for the hashtags. Searching for #ocean will find all Instagram photos with that hashtag.

CHAPTER 5

Fun with Filters

Tagging and hashtagging help users share photos. But it is the photos themselves that have set Instagram apart from similar apps and sites. Instagram's photo editing tools are extremely *robust*.

Instagram's tools include *filters*, which are its most *unique* and popular features. Filters are editing tools that can make a photo look more artistic by altering its tint, color, and more. Instagram offers 27 different filters,

Earlybird filter

Mayfair filter

Willow filter

including Earlybird, Mayfair, Willow, and Toaster.

So, a user may post a photo exactly as he or she took it. Or he or she can use a *filter* to make the photo look brighter, warmer, burn the edges, and more. A filter can transform an ordinary photo into a work of art.

Filters

Filters can alter a photo in several different ways. Filters start by breaking the full image down into pixels. Pixels are tiny units of color combinations. Together, pixels make up an image.

Instagram uses computer codes that increase or reduce specific pixel colors. This changes the way an image looks. For example, the code used in one filter may increase the color red in the image's pixels. Each filter applies specific codes that change the photo in a different way.

Toaster filter

15

CHAPTER 6

Facebook Buyout

Instagram's unique features made it wildly popular with users. This popularity did not go unnoticed by other social media companies. In 2012, several of these companies began offering to buy Instagram.

In April 2012, executives at Twitter, a social media website, offered to buy Instagram for $500 million. The Instagram founders turned it down. Soon after, Mark Zuckerberg, the founder of social media website Facebook, offered to buy Instagram for $1 billion. Systrom and Krieger took the deal.

On April 9, 2012, Facebook announced its purchase of Instagram. Usually, when one company buys another company, the buyer controls the new company. If the purchased company had been a competitor, the buyer may close the company it bought. This eliminates the competition.

Mark Zuckerberg spoke about new Instagram features at Facebook headquarters in California in 2013.

The Facebook-Instagram deal was different. Although Facebook owns Instagram, Instagram is independent. Systrom and Krieger still run the company.

CHAPTER 7

Instagram Changes

Soon after Facebook bought Instagram, the app's conditions changed. Legally, users of any social media site must agree to its conditions in order to create an account on the site. Instagram's conditions originally stated that users owned photos they took. This meant others couldn't use photos without an owner's permission.

On December 17, 2012, Instagram changed its conditions. The conditions now said businesses could pay the site to use Instagrammers' photos in advertisements. Many users were very angry about this. Some even deleted their Instagram accounts.

Instagram apologized to its users the next day. And Systrom explained that the company meant it was going to experiment with new advertising methods. It did not mean to sell or use people's photos without permission. Many users rejoined the site.

Instagram videos can be between 3 and 15 seconds long.

In 2013, Instagram made changes that its users loved. The first was adding video. The second was Instagram Direct. This feature let users share content with a small, chosen group of people, rather than making it public. Instagram Direct also allows users to chat with each other in real time.

CHAPTER 8

Creating Awareness

Instagram has become an important resource for sharing ideas, inspiration, and information. Sharing Instagram content across other social media sites plays a part in this. Instagram users can link their accounts to their Facebook pages. Users with Apple-brand devices can also link their Twitter accounts to Instagram.

Sharing and linking allows users to reach even more people and get a bigger following. Many organizations have used this as a way to bring awareness to social issues. One example is the international charity WaterAid.

In 2012, WaterAid used Instagram for its The Big Dig campaign. The organization wanted to raise money to dig boreholes in Malawi. These boreholes would improve the availability of safe drinking water there.

WaterAid staff in Malawi used Instagram to share photos and videos of the villagers' daily task of digging

for water in the ground. The photos helped encourage people to give money to the campaign. Altogether, the project raised about $3 million. In return, more than 134,000 Malawians were able to access clean water.

CHAPTER 9

Effects of Instagram

Instagram can be used to great effect in social awareness campaigns and by businesses. It can also have a great effect on individual users' lives. Users make personal connections by sharing their photos and videos. As users find other users who like the same things they do, Instagram communities form.

Instagram has also increased people's interest in photography. Looking at other users' photos gives Instagrammers ideas for their own images. It challenges them to take more creative photos.

With the increased interest in personal photography came the rise of the selfie. Instagram is credited with the booming popularity of these types of photos. Users love to share selfies on Instagram.

Posting selfies and personal photographs on sites such as Instagram can be positive or negative. Studies have

Many Instagrammers take selfies in front of monuments,
such as Big Ben in England, or other important places.

shown that social media users can form their self-images
based on others' reactions to their photos. Positive
attention and approval can create positive feelings. But
negative comments can damage a user's self-esteem.

Looking at other people's photos can also be harmful, according to a 2014 survey. When people post filtered images, they are altering reality. Followers may feel their own lives are not as good as those of the people they are following.

Instagram interactions can have a great effect. So, it is important to avoid making negative comments about others' photos. This can lead to cyberbullying.

Instagram users should also be careful about the images they share. Once an image is posted to a public account, any user can see it. Users should think twice before posting images they wouldn't want a parent or teacher to see.

Many Instagram users want to share their photos with as many people as possible. But some users only want to share photos with their friends and family members. These users can make their accounts private. Users with private accounts decide who can follow them.

Some people think Instagram users make themselves or their lives look more exciting than they really are.

CHAPTER 10

The Future of Instagram

Instagram has come a long way since its launch. It has connected people around the world and revolutionized mobile phone photography. By 2015, Instagram had more than 400 million users, and was still growing.

Instagram has also continued to introduce new features. It added the video feature Boomerang in 2015. This feature lets users take a burst of photos that are turned into a mini video. Then, this mini video can be played backward and forward.

People liked Instagram from the start because it was easier and more fun to use than other photo apps.

Silly pet photos are very popular on Instagram.

Users continue to wonder what's next for Instagram. Will new functions and filters allow them to create even more amazing photos? Instagram's leaders are constantly working on ways to improve their product. What Instagram will look like in the future is unknown. But its users' photos will certainly be part of shaping it!

Instagram

An Instagram user must be at least 13 to have an account. The first step is creating log-in information and a profile.

Once signed up, users look for accounts to follow. This includes friends' accounts or other users with interesting photos.

Users choose images to upload from their mobile devices or computers. Or, users can take photos from within the app. Users can experiment with different filters before uploading a photo.

Users can comment on others' images. It's important to be kind. Users shouldn't say mean things or bully anyone.

Users who see something scary or inappropriate should tell an adult. They can also report inappropriate content to Instagram.

It's important for users to be safe when posting to Instagram. They shouldn't use their real names as their usernames or reveal personal information, such as their home addresses.

Glossary

access – the ability or permission to enter or use a place or a thing.

apologize – to say that you are sorry about something.

availability – the quality of being able to be had or used.

borehole – a hole dug into the earth in order to find water or oil.

caption – a written explanation of an image, such as a photo.

cyberbully – to tease, hurt, or threaten someone online.

delete – to remove or eliminate.

filter – a tool that can change the appearance of a photo.

Global Positioning System (GPS) – a space-based navigation system used to pinpoint locations on Earth.

inappropriate – not suitable, fitting, or proper.

keyword – a special phrase or word that narrows an app or Internet search.

mobile – capable of moving or being moved.

negative – bad or hurtful.

permission – formal consent.

robust – strong and impressive.

self-esteem – a feeling of pride and of respect for yourself.

self-image – the way you think about yourself and your abilities or appearance.

selfie – an image of oneself taken by oneself using a digital camera, especially for posting on social networks.

server – a computer in a network that is used to provide services to other computers.

start-up – a new company started by the people who will run it.

unique (yoo-NEEK) – being the only one of its kind.

upload – to transfer data from a computer to a larger network.

Websites

To learn more about Social Media Sensations, visit **booklinks.abdopublishing.com**. These links are routinely monitored and updated to provide the most current information available.

Index